SUMMARY of Dave Asprey's HEAD STRONG:

The Bulletproof Plan to Activate Untapped Brain Energy to Work Smarter and Think Faster—in Just Two Weeks

by SUMOREADS

Copyright © 2017 by SUMOREADS. All rights reserved. This book or parts thereof may not be reproduced in any form, stored in any retrieval system, or transmitted in any form by any means—electronic, mechanical, photocopy, recording, or otherwise—without prior written permission of the publisher, except as provided by United States of America copyright law. This is an unofficial summary and is not intended as a substitute or replacement for the original book.

TABLE OF CONTENTS

EXECUTIVE SUMMARY 6

PART I: IT'S ALL IN YOUR HEAD 7
Chapter 1: Head Start
Chapter 2: Mighty Mitochondria
Chapter 3: Become a Neuromaster
Chapter 4: Inflammation

PART II: YOU ARE IN CONTROL OF YOUR HEAD
.... 10
Chapter 5: Brain Fuel
Chapter 6: Brain-Inhibiting Foods
Chapter 7: Avoid Toxins and Improve Your Body's Detox Systems
Chapter 8: Your Brain on Light, Air, and Cold
Chapter 9: Sleep Harder, Meditate Faster, Exercise Less

PART III: The Two Week Head Strong Program 14
Chapter 10: Eat to Fuel your Brain
Chapter 11: Head Strong Lifestyle
Chapter 12: Head Strong Supplements
Chapter 13: Beyond the Limits

KEY TAKEAWAYS 17
Key Takeaway: The amount of energy available to your brain directly impacts your concentration
Key Takeaway: Excessive dietary reliance on sugar for energy diminishes your ability to produce energy and leads to sugar craving
Key Takeaway: Toxins in your diet or environment decrease your brain energy levels
Key Takeaway: Mitochondria are the most important part of your bod

Key Takeaway: Early-onset mitochondrial dysfunction can have devastating health effects later

Key Takeaway: Eating the right kinds of fats strengthens your neurons and increases brain efficiency

Key Takeaway: Risk of chronic diseases can be decreased by diminishing bodily inflammatio

Key Takeaway: Inflammation is largely a response to what you eat

Key Takeaway: The types of food that lead to inflammation depend on the person, but certain products are universally inflammatory

Key Takeaway: Mold toxins are extremely toxic for your mitochondri

Key Takeaway: Cooking methods can make a healthy product unhealthy

Key Takeaway: Polyphenols are brain-boosting antioxidants

Key Takeaway: Environmental mold is also extremely harmful

Key Takeaway: Energy efficient lighting is inefficient for mitochondrial energy production

Key Takeaway: The best ways to detox

Key Takeaway: Ketosis might be our biggest evolutionary advantage

Key Takeaway: Fat is necessary for your brain

Key Takeaway: Miscommunication in neurotransmitters causes diseases

Key Takeaway: Meditation forces self-awareness upon us

Key Takeaway: Regular exercise is an antidepressant

Key Takeaway: Meditation slows the detriments of aging.

Key Takeaway: Good quality sleep requires plentiful amounts of energy

Key Takeaway: Good quality sleep requires plentiful amounts of energy
Key Takeaway: Nicotine in small doses is a brain power enhancer
Key Takeaway: Electronic stimulation is an underrated manner of maximizing brain performance

EDITORIAL REVIEW... 29
ABOUT THE AUTHOR... 31

EXECUTIVE SUMMARY

Head Strong by Dave Asprey is a book predicated on a very simple premise: that we are wasting the potential of our body, and more specifically, of our brain. The book acts as a manual and explanatory guide toward achieving the full capabilities of the human body. Asprey aims to demonstrate to everyone what he has discovered over the course of many experiments, observations, and research. He has traveled to the far corners of the world to learn from Tibetan monks and to meditate with Buddhist teachers all to understand the intricacies of science when it comes to the human body. The single greatest conclusion he comes up with is that we should aspire, as much as possible, to strengthen and build up the powerhouses of our cells: the mitochondria.

Asprey does not only show us what we should try to eat, and how we should sleep, exercise and meditate. He also illustrates the dangers that lie behind much of what we should not eat, how we should not sleep, and the way we should not spend our days. In short, he protests much of what Americans especially are prone to doing. He reveals facts and research that corroborate many of his claims and point to a cleaner, healthier, and smarter way of living. His Head Strong program specifically suggests two weeks of intense upheaval in the way we exercise, work, eat, sleep, and more generally, in the way most of us live our lives.

PART I: IT'S ALL IN YOUR HEAD

Chapter 1: Head Start

Your brain uses up to 20 percent of your body's energy and low brain energy can lead to forgetfulness, cravings, low energy, moodiness, and inability to focus. Limiting the things in your environment that sap your brain energy, adding the right diverse source of fuel for your brain energy, increasing efficiency of energy production and delivery, and strengthening your cells' mitochondria (descendants of bacteria in your cells that create energy) can allow you to hack your brain, enabling it to reach its full potential.

Chapter 2: Mighty Mitochondria

From their origin one and a half billion years ago as bacteria in an oxygen filled atmosphere to their incorporation into the cells of all living beings, mitochondria have been the source of life on Earth. They transform oxygen into energy (ATP) and allow for the functioning of all the critical systems in our bodies. Without them we would die in seconds. From age thirty to seventy, mitochondria lose 50 percent efficiency on average. Although there are no major short-term symptoms aside from mood swings, cravings and fatigue, in the long term this can lead to loss of cells, cell dehydration, a decrease in mental capacity, loss in the ability to detoxify your body, and mitochondrial decay. Though mitochondrial decay is irreversible, early-onset mitochondrial dysfunction can be reversed by paying attention to hormone and blood sugar levels as well as lifestyle and diet.

Chapter 3: Become a Neuromaster

The way your neurons functions and the connections they make are responsible for how responsive you are, and how quickly you think and learn. Neurons require a huge amount of energy to function properly and without the right amount of energy, neuronal functions become unpredictable and your neurons can die. There are many things that can be done to ensure neurons are fully functional, such as building the insulating protection around neurons called the myelin sheath, creating new neurons, and giving your neurons more power. It is also possible to grow new neurons in a process called neurogenesis. This process is highly affected by environment and lifestyle and it is important to avoid neurotoxins, stress, and depression as well as sugars and oxidized fats. On the other hand, Omega-3 fatty acids, exercise, light, water, sex, and fun environments all help neurogenesis.

Chapter 4: Inflammation

Inflammation is the body's response to stress from toxins, pathogens or trauma and it serves to heal and protect the body. Acute inflammation is healthy and necessary and allows new muscle growth. It is only problematic when it's chronic and your entire body is inflamed. Having the right balance of bacteria in your digestive tract, ensuring you have the right hormonal balance, having sufficient exposure to light, and making sure you have enough water in your system will diminish mitochondrial inflammation and increase energy production. This will ensure your brain is higher functioning and decreases your likelihood of developing chronic diseases down the road.

PART II: YOU ARE IN CONTROL OF YOUR HEAD

Chapter 5: Brain Fuel

Nutrition is the single greatest influence over how your brain is powered. The mitochondria in your body cells need oxygen to make ATP, but within that energy-making process, free radicals are created, which "cause havoc in your cells." In order to counter that, you need to eat your vegetables, since they contain antioxidants, and more specifically, you need to eat polyphenols, carefully choose your inhibitory neurotransmitters, and ingest certain types of beneficial fat. At the same time, we should also aim to be in intermittent ketosis (in a later chapter he demonstrates the best ways to do so)—a state achieved in periods of fast or starvation.

Chapter 6: Brain-Inhibiting Foods

Your diet and the products you expose your body to can both help your brain capacity and damage it. Certain foods can lead to inflammation of your digestive tract and lead your immune system to attack healthy cells, consuming excessive energy and minimizing your brain power. Each immune system is different and can react differently to different food types. However, some foods lead to inflammation for nearly everybody. There are two kinds of toxins that come from your food. The ones that manufacturers add to products such as pesticides, preservatives and artificial flavors, and the natural ones made to protect plants and fungi from the living creatures that consume them. Mold toxins which are found in grains, wine, beer, coffee, dried fruit, chocolate, nuts and corn are particularly damaging to your mitochondria and even initially healthy products can become detrimental due to the cooking method used.

Chapter 7: Avoid Toxins and Improve Your Body's Detox Systems

Many people throw around the term "detox" but what does detoxing actually mean? There are many kinds of toxins that are harmful to the brain, and detoxing is a crucial component in taking care of and optimizing your brain. Toxins can induce toxic stress, which kill or damage mitochondria, which can then kill or damage your neurons, creating a vicious cycle. Asprey goes on to describe the dangers of environmental mold, which can quickly spread, and are noticeably harmful to your normal performance. To fight both environmental mold, food mold, and the toxins present in heavy metals like lead or mercury, Asprey recommends sticking to the Head Start nutritional plan which will constantly help you detox. He also lays out his skepticism of many pharmaceutical drugs that can be harmful to your mitochondria (he also acknowledges that these drugs are life-saving for others).

Chapter 8: Your Brain on Light, Air, and Cold

Light, air and temperature are among the most essential components of life on Earth. Our contemporary environment gives us unnatural and unhealthy exposure to these critical components. Light is a nutrient that is very important to mitochondrial function. After the brain and the heart (and the ovaries for women), the eyes have the highest concentration of mitochondria as our visual system requires 15 percent of our body's total energy. Forcing your eyes to work in an environment with unnatural light frequencies damages mitochondria and energy production and decreases ability to process visual information. Similarly, oxygen is arguably the most vital component of life and energy production, and we are living in an environment with ever lower oxygen levels. However, it is possible to increase the efficiency of our oxygen intake by periodically limiting it over short periods in order to kill off weak mitochondria and strengthen the well well-functioning ones. Finally, when your body is exposed to cold it is forced to create heat in a process called thermogenesis. This process burns fat and reduces inflammation, which is why ice packs are used in injuries and why occasional bodily exposure to the cold can increase brain and overall body performance.

Chapter 9: Sleep Harder, Meditate Faster, Exercise Less

In this chapter, Asprey delineates the ways to improve efficiency and performance by maximizing sleep, meditating more effectively, and exercising less. Most people think that sleep is a time to rest the body and brain, but in truth the brain is still working at high capacity to clean up the day's work. This cleanup is powered by the mitochondria, therefore, if your mitochondria is strong and healthy then the cleanup time will be finished quicker, and you'll need less time to sleep. That sleep will still be of high quality, however. Meditation is also key to sleep, but it also creates more folds in the outer layer of the brain, which has been shown to demonstrate more intelligence. Naturally, it also helps strengthen your mitochondria in a way that causes you to experience decreased stress, and reductions in infertility and depression. Finally, exercise is something that we all know to be healthy, but it doesn't only get you in shape, it also strengthens your mitochondria, and helps them make energy faster. While exercise is undoubtedly beneficial, we should seek to do it in short, intense spurts rather than long daily sessions. Though counter to common beliefs about how much exercise is the right amount, Asprey's research has concluded that less frequent, but more intense exercise is best.

PART III:
THE TWO WEEK HEAD STRONG PROGRAM

Chapter 10: Eat to Fuel your Brain

It is not necessary to have a low-calorie diet for it to be healthy. On the contrary, since calories are used to measure energy you will need plenty for your brain to function at maximum efficiency. The first step is buying the right products. Local, organic produce will always be the best choice. Then, Dave Asprey offers a series of recipes that will ensure brain efficiency and overall bodily health. From lamb and cucumber burgers to coconut-lamb curry, Asprey proposes a series of recipes that will be sure to keep you fed and energetic throughout the day.

Chapter 11: Head Strong Lifestyle

In order to get the full benefits of the Head Strong program, you might need to change your lifestyle. You can start with simple changes to your light and cold exposure, as well as sleep, meditation, and exercise to allow your mitochondria to make the most of the nutritional fuel you are now providing your brain. You should block LED lights, change your electronics settings to minimize blue light, dim your electric lights, make your bedroom as dark as possible, even wear sunglasses inside, and aim to expose your skin to natural light and not artificial light as much as possible. Practice what Asprey calls "meaningful movement" combined with high-intensity workouts, and resistance once a week. Learn to "hack" your sleep, by switching to decaf coffee after 2 p.m., not working out before sleep, knowing and following your chronotype, eating a spoonful of honey before bed, while also remembering to go into Airplane Mode on your electronics, and to perform breathing exercises as you lie down before sleeping. Finally, meditate regularly—there are a number of techniques and different methods to test to see which fits you best.

Chapter 12: Head Strong Supplements

Though taking supplements is not necessary to strengthen your mitochondria, they can make it much easier to overcome particular obstacles and to reach your mitochondrial full potential. Asprey divides supplements into three categories; low-impact supplements that are generally cheaper and have long-term benefits (such as caffeine, vitamin B12, magnesium, vitamin D3), medium impact supplements that have a growing impact over time (creatine, krill oil, polyphenol blend, sprout extract) and high-impact supplements that have maximum and immediate impact on your energy levels (ketoprime, glutathione, activepqq).

Chapter 13: Beyond the Limits

After completing the two-week Head Strong program, if you are satisfied and wish to make your performance even more efficient, Asprey offers a series of more expensive, more extreme methods to increase brain energy. Transcranial magnetic stimulation for example involves sending magnetic pulses to your brain while you sleep, which releases serotonin, melatonin and other neurotransmitters that are necessary for a healthy night sleep. Sleeping on a mat with spikes that are not painful but uncomfortable forces your fight or flight reflex to be intensely stimulated, which allows you to relax more easily, once you become used to the discomfort. Ozone therapy, cryotherapy (standing in cold air that is -270 degrees Fahrenheit for up to three minutes) are other expensive treatments that boost your brain performance. For simpler biohacks, Asprey recommends shaking, bouncing, and making your body vibrate to make the water in your body move, while decreasing inflammation. Other hacks can be as simple as walking barefoot, or training your eyes and ears to become accustomed to the sensory overload you face in your daily environments.

KEY TAKEAWAYS

Key Takeaway: The amount of energy available to your brain directly impacts your concentration

When your brain is low on energy, it stimulates the release of the stress hormone called cortisol that breaks down muscle to make the pancreas release the insulin required to metabolize sugar, which in turn requires energy and creates a state of brain emergency that releases more cortisol. Excess of this cycle leads to insulin resistance which makes glucose absorption more difficult. This in turn forces your brain to constantly jump in and out of fight or flight mode and thus makes you unable to focus on a given task for more than a few seconds.

Key Takeaway: Excessive dietary reliance on sugar for energy diminishes your ability to produce energy and leads to sugar cravings

Mitochondria use oxygen to burn fat, glucose or amino acids to make energy. If you eat too much sugar your mitochondria cannot produce energy from fat as effectively, which means they receive their fuel from glucose. This leads to sugar crashes and food cravings—of which the desire for sugar is most prominent. It is therefore important to eat enough of the right kind of fat to not be overly reliant on sugar.

Key Takeaway: Toxins in your diet or environment decrease your brain energy levels

Consuming something toxic to your body sends alarms for extra sugar to oxidize or metabolize the toxins and thus neutralize them. The same occurs to counteract negative external stimuli such as noise or bad lighting. The result is a significant decrease in brain energy.

Key Takeaway: Mitochondria are the most important part of your body

The average cell contains 1000–2000 mitochondria, meaning you have more than a quadrillion mitochondria in your body. Aside from allowing oxygen to be transformed into energy in what is known as the Krebs cycle, they are responsible for cellular differentiation, control of cell growth and death cycles as well as transmitting signals between cells. Cells in the brain, heart and retina have the most mitochondria and suffer first from lack of energy supply. Mitochondria deterioration occurs with old age and is accelerated by improper diet and excessive environmental toxin exposure, but it is not fatal.

Key Takeaway: Early-onset mitochondrial dysfunction can have devastating health effects later

Loss in mitochondrial numbers or efficiency can lead to many health issues and brain deficiency. However, it is possible to ensure your body's mitochondria do not deteriorate and thus avoid early-onset mitochondrial dysfunction (EOMD), discovered by Dr. Shallenberger and defined as when mitochondrial function deteriorates in people under 40. He estimates 46 percent of people have EOMD. The leading causes of EOMD are improper nutrient intake, excessive stress, hormonal deficiencies, and exposure to environmental toxins.

Key Takeaway: Eating the right kinds of fats strengthens your neurons and increases brain efficiency

Neurons are enveloped in a protective layer of fat that ensures the transmission of electrical signals along the neuron, called the myelin sheath. Though at birth we have very little myelin, it is rapidly built during infancy—one of the main reasons babies develop so rapidly. Myelin is much harder to restore than it is to be kept strong. It relies on having the right balance of hormones to restore itself. Myelin is made of made of saturated fat, cholesterol, omega-3 fatty acids and omega-6 fatty acids, which is why Western medicine's war on cholesterol has been misguided. Eating enough of the right kinds of fat is crucial. Insufficient cholesterol consumption leads to a decrease in brain functions such as memory and can lead to Alzheimer's. Diets mimicking the effects of fasting can also help myelination.

Key Takeaway: Risk of chronic diseases can be decreased by diminishing bodily inflammation

Today, cardiovascular disease, cancer and diabetes are responsible for nearly 70 percent of all deaths in the United States and they are all linked to bodily inflammation. Inflammation is caused by things that irritate the body, such as physical or psychological stress. When any part of the body is inflamed, cytokines are released and negatively affect your brain. When your mitochondria are inflamed, electrons used to create energy have to travel further and energy production is less efficient. All decreases in energy production now eventually lead to chronic diseases later. Many of the symptoms of old age such as forgetfulness, decreased learning ability and loss in concentration are due to non-pathological brain (and particularly prefrontal cortex) inflammation.

Key Takeaway: Inflammation is largely a response to what you eat

Approximately 50 percent of the body's immune system is located in the digestive tract. When immune cells encounter a foreign molecule the body produces inflammation, experienced as bloating and brain fog. Anything fried or charred will systematically cause inflammation. The fewer types of bacteria you have in your digestive tract, the more your immune system is weakened and the higher your chance of getting Alzheimer's and other chronic diseases. Therefore, taking too many antibiotics can upset the bacterial balance in your digestive tract, which can also lead to inflammation. Nonetheless, it is still important to consume the right kind of fats. Omega-6 fatty acids are pro-inflammatory fats whereas Omega-3 fatty acids are anti-inflammatory fats. Omega-6 fatty acids are mainly found in vegetable oils which are the cheapest source of fat calories in the world and can be found in most packaged foods.

Key Takeaway: The types of food that lead to inflammation depend on the person, but certain products are universally inflammatory

Though a blood test is the best way to know your personal bodily sensitivities it is possible to know by measuring your heart rate. When you consume a product your body is sensitive to, your heart rate increases by approximately seventeen beats per minute within ninety minutes of eating. There are also certain types of products to be avoided by everyone. Trans fats for example, which manufacturers like to use because they conserve longer than other types of fats, are devastating for your immune system as are dairy products, gluten, and vegetable oils.

Key Takeaway: Mold toxins are extremely toxic for your mitochondria

What's more, they are much more prevalent than we assume. A 2016 study found that 96 percent of grain samples contain at least ten types of mycotoxin (mold toxins). So not only are grains bad for your health, but products coming from animals that eat grain are too. Coffee has significant amounts of mold toxins and most countries have set strict regulations of coffee mold toxin levels, which the United States has not. In fact, any coffee shipment that does not meet the regulations in these countries is sent to the United States. Dried fruit, nuts, beer, wine and corn are also high in mold toxins.

Key Takeaway: Cooking methods can make a healthy product unhealthy

The methods with which you cook an initially healthy food can turn it into a mitochondria slowing product that causes inflammation and significant brain energy loss. Smoking, frying or grilling meat create two different types of carcinogens which not only cause cancer but are also neurotoxic. Furthermore, certain cooking methods such as frying, or barbecuing using vegetable or cooking oils also denatures proteins and fats, turning a perfectly healthy product into a high energy consuming one.

Key Takeaway: Polyphenols are brain-boosting antioxidants

All vegetables have antioxidants in some way, shape or form, but polyphenols are a specific type of antioxidant that can protect against cellular damage from oxidation and a few other things. They also protect your gut by increasing the quantity of healthy bacteria while limiting damaging bacteria in your intestinal tract which can reduce brain fog; they augment your rate of neurogenesis which can help learning, memory, and thinking; they better modulate when your cells live and die to maximize their output; and finally, they reduce the number of inflammatory cytokines in your bloodstream to improve blood flow to the brain.

Key Takeaway: Environmental mold is also extremely harmful

28 percent of people have a genetic sensibility to mold, which can lead to brain fog, cognitive issues, fatigue, joint pain, nausea, weight gain, chronic sinusitis, and asthma. However, the rest of the population can also feel these symptoms on a lower scale, which inhibits performance in much the way being hungover does. If you take an IQ test before and after exposure to mold, you can suffer a decrease of up to 15 IQ points after exposure.

Key Takeaway: Energy efficient lighting is inefficient for mitochondrial energy production

The sun emits light on multiple frequencies of the light spectrum including the invisible infrared and ultraviolet frequencies. Today we block infrared and ultraviolet light (through UV-filtering windows, sunglasses and windshields) partly for good reason as overexposure to ultraviolet light can lead to sunburns and cancer or eye damage. However, UV light is necessary to activate vitamin D and regulate your sleeping patterns. Similarly, the lights that we use to illuminate our homes, offices and screens use the most energy efficient form of light known as "blue light" which can lead to short sightedness and brain energy deficiency while having a negative effect on sleep patterns.

Key Takeaway: The best ways to detox

There are a few ways to eliminate the harmful toxins in your body, and sweating in a sauna is a very easy one. It can be achieved through exercise too, but sweating it out in a sauna is better. Another is called chelation therapy, which intravenously introduces chelators in your bloodstream to bind with toxins, allowing you to pass them normally. Finally, there is also chlorella, which works particularly well for heavy metal exposure.

Key Takeaway: Ketosis might be our biggest evolutionary advantage

Ketosis is the state whereby we enter into a state of high performance induced by starvation or fasting. During these periods of fasting or severe carbohydrate limitation, the liver produces what are called ketone bodies by breaking down fatty acids. These ketone bodies are a consummate source of nutrition for the mitochondria. We get 28 percent more brain energy when we are in ketosis. Without ketosis, we would die of starvation when we do not have enough food, but thanks to it, we actually augment our productivity! Humans are the only animals that enter ketosis precisely because our brains are so large, and we need the ketones to protect our brains from the harmful oxidation that would otherwise happen. Without ketones, we would die of starvation within six days. However, if you maintain a state of ketosis for too long, you start feeling nauseated, while also losing in sleep quality, as well as in general productivity.

Key Takeaway: Fat is necessary for your brain

A diet that contains a large amount of healthy fats aids in lowering inflammation throughout your body and increasing energy production in your brain. In fact, our bodies are quite literally composed of fat—a healthy woman is usually made up of 25–29 percent fat, while a healthy man hovers around 15–20 percent fat. Our brains contain the most fat, which is why they can convert energy so efficiently when we eat healthy fats. People often worry that eating fats will put more cholesterol in their body, which is actually a good thing if the cholesterol taken is high-density lipoprotein (HDL) as opposed to low-density lipoprotein (LDL). The former allows your body to get rid of the latter, which is harmful, and more importantly, having a low count of HDL has been shown to lead to neurodegenerative diseases, and cognitive impairment. The best sources of fat are grass-fed animal meat and fat, grass-fed beef tallow, pastured egg yolks, olive oil, wild caught low-mercury seafood, and fish/krill oil.

Key Takeaway: Miscommunication in neurotransmitters causes diseases

Neurotransmitters are the messengers that allow neurons to communicate with one another. Nearly everything that the body does can be traced back to neurotransmitters, so they are vitally important. Neurotransmitters can be inhibited when taken in too large or little quantities of things like dopamine (found in cocaine, opium, alcohol and heroin), norepinephrine (beef, chicken, turkey, bacon, avocados), serotonin (antidepressants, and hallucinogens), L-tryptophan (lamb, beef, chicken, cashews, almonds, hazelnuts, wild salmon), acetylcholine (beef, lamb, pork, egg yolk, liver), and gamma-aminobutyric acid (beef, lamb, chicken, turkey, wild salmon, eggs, organ meats). A lot of these lists have a great deal of overlap, and that is because these are some of the best nutrients that we can eat—if taken in the right doses.

Key Takeaway: Meditation forces self-awareness upon us

If we all meditated 10 minutes every single day, we would all come out feeling happier, fresher, healthier, and more positive. The reason for that is that meditation focuses energy upon ourselves, and we take a moment to stop and think about our thoughts, our actions, to control the erratic wild swings that come every so often to all of us.

Key Takeaway: Regular exercise is an antidepressant

Regular exercise can be "at least as powerful as antidepressants in fighting depression." It also strengthens the mitochondria and eliminates the toxins that can be harmful to your body. However, exercise doesn't have to come in the traditional gym workout we think of—it can come through yoga, a simple walk, or endurance training. If you do perform high-intensity workouts regularly, be sure to include several days or rest in between them to recover.

Key Takeaway: Meditation slows the detriments of aging

With meditation, the outer layer of our brains thickens, which means that with age, they flatten less quickly, allowing us to maintain our problem-solving skills, our bodily awareness and our concentration.

Key Takeaway: Good quality sleep requires plentiful amounts of energy

When you wake up between 3 and 5 a.m. and can't get back to sleep it's usually an indicator that your blood sugar is too low, which causes cortisol release that wakes you up. A healthy snack before going to bed can ensure your body has enough energy for a quality night of rest.

Key Takeaway: Good quality sleep requires plentiful amounts of energy

When you wake up between 3 and 5 a.m. and are unable to get back to sleep it is usually an indicator that your blood sugar is too low, which causes a cortisol release that wakes you up. A healthy snack before going to bed can ensure your body has enough energy for a quality night of rest.

Key Takeaway: Nicotine in small doses is a brain power enhancer

Nicotine particularly when not wrapped in the carcinogenic products in cigarettes is beneficial to your brain. It accelerates your motor function, makes you more vigilant, gives you greater brain stamina as well as short-term memory. However, the negative effect of addiction must be kept into account as tobacco was found to be the third most addictive drug after cocaine and heroin. The solution is to take small doses via nicotine gum or spray which contain 5–20 percent of the nicotine in an industrial cigarette.

Key Takeaway: Electronic stimulation is an underrated manner of maximizing brain performance

A hundred years ago there was a big debate within the scientific community as to whether the body was chemical or electric. The chemical side won the argument which explains the explosion of "big pharma" but in reality, the body is much more complex and the chemical and electrical are two sides of the same coin. As such, electrical stimulation such as cranial electrotherapy (developed by the Russian space program to cut costs by training astronauts to perform better with less sleep) can act as a mitochondria supercharger.

EDITORIAL REVIEW

Head Strong by Dave Asprey is a book centered around hacking your brain, and maximizing the potential that each and every one of us can achieve. For the last decade or so, Asprey has collaborated with leading doctors and scientists to uncover the latest scientific methods behind increasing brain performance. The book is rife with research studies and innovative tools that aim to create a two-week regime—the Head Strong program—that anyone can follow. Throughout the text, one can sense Asprey's obsession with enhancing performance, and elevating brain cognition, both in the short and long term. There is scarcely a single aspect of our daily life and routine that he leaves out. According to Asprey, everything can be "hacked." He focuses the vast majority of his innovative exercises and tools on boosting and strengthening the mitochondria, the famous powerhouse of the cell—and therefore, of the brain. His passion for heightening our performance is infectious, and throughout the book the reader is easily seduced by the prospect of achieving that elusive state of mind and body. It is also clear that Asprey writes from firsthand experience, having experimented with everything that he describes and analyzes.

However, this book is not necessarily easy reading either. A science-oriented individual may be able to intuitively follow many of the processes he describes, but anyone else might find the content within to be dense and hard to follow. Part of the appeal of this project is the fact that it is based upon research and scientific revelations, yet to all who might think that this is a beachside read, beware, for you are about to embark on a journey into a complex detailing of the chemical and electrical processes of the human body. Even so, there are different ways to enjoy this book, and reading every single line need not be one of them. Asprey seems to have recognized that the fine lines of his explanations are not for everyone. At the end of every chapter he has condensed the most important points and actionable insights into several bullet points, which can be invaluable to the less scientifically inclined among us.

All in all, this book is rife with fascinating, eye-opening revelations that could, without exaggeration, turn out to be life-changing for some. For those who do decide to read a few pages of this manual for "hacking your brain," you will surely never think of your body and the things we do with it in the same way.

ABOUT THE AUTHOR

Dave Asprey is a Silicon Valley technology entrepreneur, creating products like Bulletproof Coffee made with butter, while also writing *New York Times* bestselling books, and generally searching for new and innovative ways of biohacking. He also hosts *Bulletproof Radio*, a Webby Award-winning podcast, with 50 million downloads. He has appeared on *Nightline*, CNN and in the *Financial Times*, *GQ*, *Men's Fitness*, *Rolling Stone*, *Men's Health*, *Vogue*, the *New York Times*, and *Forbes*, along with many others.

He currently lives in Victoria, British Columbia, and Seattle, Washington.

THE END

If you enjoyed this summary, please leave an honest review on Amazon.com…it'd mean a lot to us.

If you haven't already, we encourage you to purchase a copy of the original book.

Made in the USA
Middletown, DE
25 October 2017